W9-BIH-864

ALL ABOUT FALL

Pumpkin Harvest

by Calvin Harris

Consulting Editor: Gail Saunders-Smith, PhD

Capstone press®

Mankato, Minnesota

Pebble Plus is published by Capstone Press,
151 Good Counsel Drive, P.O. Box 669, Mankato, Minnesota 56002.
www.capstonepress.com

1 2 3 4 5 6 12 11 10 09 08 07

Library of Congress Cataloging-in-Publication Data
Harris, Calvin, 1980–
    Pumpkin harvest / by Calvin Harris.
    p. cm.—(Pebble plus. All about fall)
    Summary: "Simple text and photographs present the fall pumpkin harvest"—Provided by publisher.
    Includes bibliographical references and index.
    ISBN-13: 978-1-4296-0026-2 (hardcover)
    ISBN-10: 1-4296-0026-8 (hardcover)
    1. Pumpkin—Harvesting—Juvenile literature. I. Title. II. Series.
SB347.H37 2008
635'.62—dc22   2006102056

Editorial Credits
Sarah L. Schuette, editor; Veronica Bianchini, designer; Charlene Deyle, photo researcher

Photo Credits
Capstone Press/Karon Dubke, 1, 5, 13, 15, 17, 19, 21
Dreamstime/Sandra Cunningham, cover
Getty Images Inc./Stone/Paul Chesley, 11
Shutterstock/J. Gatherum, 9; Rob Byron, 7

Pebble Plus thanks Emma Krumbees in Belle Plaine, Minnesota, Sponsel's Minnesota Harvest in Jordan, Minnesota,
    and the Minnesota Landscape Arboretum in Chaska, Minnesota, for the use of their locations during photo shoots.

Note to Parents and Teachers

The All about Fall set supports national science standards related to changes during the
seasons. This book describes and illustrates the fall pumpkin harvest. The images support
early readers in understanding the text. The repetition of words and phrases helps early
readers learn new words. This book also introduces early readers to subject-specific
vocabulary words, which are defined in the Glossary section. Early readers may need
assistance to read some words and to use the Table of Contents, Glossary, Read More,
Internet Sites, and Index sections of the book.

Table of Contents

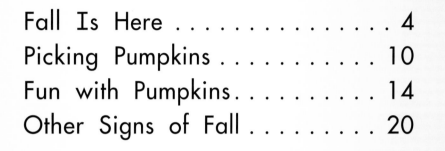

Fall Is Here

It's fall.

The weather outside

feels cool and crisp.

5

Orange pumpkins
fill a patch of land.
They grow on green vines
near the ground.

The vines turn brown
and dry up.
It's time to harvest
the pumpkins.

Picking Pumpkins

Farmers cut the ripe pumpkins from their vines.

They set the pumpkins out
for shoppers to buy.

Fun with Pumpkins

Pumpkins make fall
a fun time.
They make good heads
for scarecrows.

Pumpkins are scooped out
to make jack-o-lanterns.

Pumpkins are baked

into sweet pumpkin pies.

Other Signs of Fall

The pumpkin harvest
has begun.
What are other signs
that it's fall?

Glossary

harvest—to gather or pick crops that are ripe

jack-o-lantern—a pumpkin with a face carved into it; jack-o-lanterns are Halloween decorations.

patch—a small piece of land or field where pumpkins grow

ripe—ready to be picked or eaten

scarecrow—a figure made of straw that looks like a person; scarecrows are used to scare birds away from crops.

vine—a plant with a long stem that grows along the ground; pumpkins grow on vines.

Read More

Ghigna, Charles. *Oh My, Pumpkin Pie!* Step into Reading. New York: Random House, 2005.

Jones, Christianne C. *Autumn Orange.* Know Your Colors. Minneapolis: Picture Window Books, 2006.

Pfeffer, Wendy. *We Gather Together: Celebrating the Harvest Season.* New York: Dutton Children's Books, 2006.

Internet Sites

FactHound offers a safe, fun way to find Internet sites related to this book. All of the sites on FactHound have been researched by our staff.

Here's how:

1. Visit *www.facthound.com*

2. Choose your grade level.

3. Type in this book ID **1429600268** for age-appropriate sites. You may also browse subjects by clicking on letters, or by clicking on pictures and words.

4. Click on the **Fetch It** button.

FactHound will fetch the best sites for you!

Index

Word Count: 92
Grade: 1
Early-Intervention Level: 12